Victor Lustig: The Life and Legacy of the 20ᵗʰ Century's Most Notorious Con Artist

By Charles River Editors

"Count" Victor Lustig, in center (even the title is bogus), is shown being questioned by Robert L. Godby (right), U. S. agent in charge in New York, and Peter A. Rubano, Secret Service Agent, concerning the $52,000 counterfeit money found cached in a subway locker at Times Square. Other agents described Lustig as the "slickest bunko man who ever lived." Picture by Evening Journal

EVENING PUBLIC LEDGER—PHILADELPHIA,

Introduction

"Never pry into a person's personal circumstances (they'll tell you all eventually)." – "The Ten Commandments for Con Men," attributed to Victor Lustig

The art of the confidence trick is a controversial craft that is as old as time itself. In the early years of civilization, unscrupulous folks bottled and peddled assortments of fake cures and potions. Snake oil salesmen aside, charlatans posed as mystical beings with supernatural powers, promising to end droughts and other misfortunes of the gullible with what were in reality parlor tricks and illusions.

Indeed, throughout history, unabashedly brazen characters managed to make careers out of deception. 17th century Britain, for instance, was terrorized by William Chaloner, the most infamous serial counterfeiter and con artist of his time before he was ultimately bested by Sir Isaac Newton himself. The British trickster posed as a quack doctor and a clairvoyant who dispensed false fortunes (most likely via an early form of cold reading) and bogus healing antidotes, but these were bush-league frauds in comparison to one of his most renowned claims to fame: he once bribed four Jacobite sympathizers to crank out pamphlets regarding King James II's denunciation of His Royal Highness William, and later double-crossed his co-conspirators by tipping off the cops and swiftly decamping with the $1,000 reward.

Confidence women were equally active players in such dirty, fixed games. Doris Payne was a professional pilferer of jewels whose unconventional vocation spanned six decades. Throughout all her hits across the United States, Europe, and Asia, Payne adhered to a simple, yet effective method of operation: she donned stylish, pricey clothes, singled out impressionable male shopkeepers and distracted them with flirtatious small talk, and secretly palmed jewelry with sleight-of-hand tricks. One of the most recent was Frank Abagnale, a career impersonator, former forger of bank checks turned FBI employee, and the subject of the 2002 film *Catch Me If You Can*.

Despite several famous con men, there is one con man in particular who, despite being frequently overshadowed by various counterparts, managed to pull off capers so audacious that they seemed to come straight out of an adventure thriller. As a matter of fact, the mystery man in question, Victor Lustig, has often been credited with authoring the figurative handbook that modern-day con artists continue to rely on, and his story has been studied or described in countless works of literature, most notably Robert Greene's *48 Laws of Power*. Lustig was a notorious master of deception, a dangerously charismatic and conniving fellow, and could boast of exploits as incredible as selling the Eiffel Tower, not once, but twice.

Victor Lustig: The Life and Legacy of the 20th Century's Most Notorious Con Artist profiles one of the most eccentric personalities of his age. Along with pictures of important people, places, and events, you will learn about Victor Lustig like never before.

Making a Mountebank

"Nothing ventured, nothing gained." – Old Czech Proverb

As dishonorable as it was, street hustling was – if executed properly – a potentially profitable trade, and it had become something of an art form by the 19th century. Among the most popular tricks of the trade was the "drop swindle," a crafty ruse most commonly employed in the United States and across the European continent. It relied on an unsuspecting man sauntering down the street, perhaps whistling a jaunty tune, when he spots a plump wallet tumbling to the ground from the corner of his eye. He stops in his tracks, dives into the flurry of moving feet, and attempts to fish out the wallet, but is deterred by another outstretched hand. Unbeknownst to him, the other Good Samaritan had laid the bait himself, and the wallet had been stuffed with a wad of invalid, counterfeit cash. Rather than deliberate over who had stumbled upon the wallet first and therefore had dibs, the "dropper," who claims to be running late, suggests that the dupe keep the wallet and collect the reward money from the rightful owner later in return for a smaller sum of money, or some other valuable. On occasion, the patsy would fork over what they believe to be a fraction of the incoming reward money, and the Good Samaritan would disappear into the crowd. The patsy, unable to track down the owner of the wallet, will attempt to seek consolation in the cash inside the wallet, only to realize that the money is no good anywhere. It is only then that the fog is lifted, but by then, the swindler was long gone.

Across the street, a steadily swelling crowd of onlookers may have surrounded a circle of players in the midst of a round of Three Card Monte. The objective of the game is straightforward enough: the bettor must locate the red queen in the trio of cards shuffled by the dealer. Unfortunately for the bettor in question, the game is rigged, designed so as to ensure the house's victory. What's more, the dealer is not the sole manipulator - pulling the strings alongside him is a roper, responsible for reeling in victims, a lookout, tasked with sounding the alarm when a police officer is sighted, and one or two shills disguised as players themselves.

Even those familiar with the scam are at the mercy of these street swindlers. In the event that the player actually places a bet on the correct card, one of the shills makes certain to place an even higher bet on another card. The dealer then claims that only one bet may be placed a time, and when the shill refuses to withdraw their bet, the dealer is left with "no choice" but to restart the round. Shills may also choose to "inadvertently" slam into the table, or the remaining deck of cards, thereby nullifying the round. The lookout or the dealer themselves may also conveniently spot approaching police officers in the distance, causing bettors and onlookers alike to scatter in all directions at once.

Indeed, these aforementioned scams and other similar stunts were some of the most universally prevalent rackets back in the day. While these rackets, ethics aside, were moderately lucrative if executed properly, they were small-time, penny-ante hustles compared to those perpetrated by

Victor Lustig, a supremely slick and incomparably cunning master of deception who is often touted as the greatest con artist of the early 20th century.

Lustig was in many ways the antithesis of the stereotypical grifter. He took pride in his appearance and was always impeccably groomed, sporting the finest well-tailored suits, complete with his trademark Homburg hat, stylish walking cane, and dress shoes to match. At the same time, he gave wide berth to the fine line between fashionable and gaudy, making certain to never draw too much unnecessary attention to himself. Lustig was wildly charismatic and approachable, yet he was soft-spoken and selected his words carefully, which allowed him to appeal to and procure the trust of people from all walks of life.

Above all, what truly set Lustig apart from other petty crooks was his self-discipline and iron ambition. He did not chase after easy money, but instead hatched devious long cons that allowed him to rake in enormous profits. Moreover, he went on to assume at least 45 aliases (intricate backstories included) in his lifetime and notched up close to 50 arrests in a span of 16 years. Through it all, his stints behind bars did nothing to dissuade him from drawing even further outside of the lines.

The life of Victor Lustig is, in a nutshell, an action-packed story of adventure, excitement, and intrigue, but in the same breath, it also serves as a cautionary tale for those who hero-worship such glorified cheats. This is because, even when things seem to be going swimmingly, consistently weaving a web of lies is as vexatious as the threads are gossamer-thin. It is a lesson in the volatility of artifice and subterfuge, and Lustig's career demonstrates how even a single misstep or error in judgment, as well as breaching the unspoken cardinal rule of forming attachments, can lead to the brewing of a perfect storm, one that even the mightiest and most elusive of individuals cannot conquer.

There was a certain irony in Lustig's surname, which is the German term for "funny" or "ridiculous." Although the word might be applicable when describing some of his greatest schemes, objectively speaking, Lustig's victims undoubtedly failed to find even a smidgen of humor in his exploits.

Moreover, it should come as little surprise that little is known about Lustig's childhood and formative years, which is typical for a con artist. Most of the need to be taken with a grain of salt, for they were taken from the recollections of a known liar: Lustig himself. Aside from his claims, there were accounts coming from his surviving relatives and others who claim to have known him. The narrative and anecdotes spun by Lustig were also often contradictory, who he presumably offered whatever curated backstory best served his agenda at the time.

What Lustig's actual name was is still a matter of debate. According to his death certificate, the man known today as Victor Lustig was born Robert V. Miller, but in other accounts, he was christened Victor (or Viktor) Lustig at birth, and it was this surname that his descendants later adopted. Likewise, Lustig's date of birth and his birthplace also remain matters of speculation.

According to most sources, he was born on January 4, 1890 in Austria-Hungarian Arnau, or what is now the town of Hostinné in the Czech Republic. Arnau was a small, quietly elegant village set against the foothills of the seasonally snow-dusted Krkonoše Mountains, with a handsome central square dominated by a tasteful peach-colored clock tower from the Baroque period. It was a place that exuded history, with its early years marked by sieges, a catastrophic fire, and a Renaissance-style resurgence, and the place still carried the vestiges of its medieval phase. By the late 19th century, however, Arnau had mostly faded into the background, a relatively prosperous, yet uneventful village whose main claim to fame was its blossoming paper production and processing industry. Whether the monotony of his hometown played a factor – and if so, to what extent – in the shaping of Lustig's thrill-thirsting nature is certainly something to ponder.

Lustig, it seemed, could not agree with himself about his father's line of work, or where his family ranked on the social scale. At times, a twinkly-eyed, beaming Lustig claimed that his father, Ludwig Lustig, had been the mayor or *burgomaster* of Arnau, and depending on the circumstances, he either hinted at or drew specific attention to his comfortable, upper-middle class background, as well as his alleged ties to nobility. Before Ludwig, who was of mixed German, Swiss, and Czech ancestry, was elected *burgomaster*, he was a well-heeled merchant – professionally based in Prague and personally in Zurich – who dealt in tobacco and smoking pipes for a living.

Lustig's prison records, on the other hand, painted an entirely different picture of his upbringing. He claimed to have emerged from humble beginnings, and he once described his mother and father as the "poorest peasant people" who labored tirelessly in the fields, their fingers permanently riddled with cuts and callouses, just to keep a pitiful, but functioning roof over their heads. His family did not reside in a country manor, as spacious as it was stately, but rather a wretched stone cottage furnished only with the bare essentials. Due to his family's indigence, Lustig developed sticky fingers at a very young age, and he began to swipe and pocket money, jewelry, and other valuables to help cover the endless bills, though he insisted that he had only targeted the "greedy and the dishonest." In essence, he portrayed himself as something akin to a self-serving Robin Hood.

Precisely which of these accounts, which sit on opposite ends of the spectrum, is accurate or most closely resembled Lustig's actual childhood is a secret, one of many that died with him. For most of his life, Lustig proposed the former version of his childhood as fact, perhaps in a bid to aggrandize himself to influential figures and potential moneyed marks. That being said, the latter version he propagated in his later years must not be disregarded, since poverty is often an effective blade that sharpens unparalleled ambition and drive. If Lustig had indeed fabricated the latter tale, he may have done so strategically, as inmates typically do not take kindly to the privileged.

Whatever the case, by all accounts, Lustig was an exceptionally bright and adaptable child whose maturity and insight were years ahead of his peers. He was aware of his intellect and gift of perception, as well as his remarkable ability to educate himself on whatever piqued his curiosity, yet he never seemed to crave any extra attention. Even as a boy, as per the accounts of Lustig's daughter and relatives, he was strong-willed and impervious to peer pressure, seemingly indifferent to the juvenile hijinks wreaked by other lads his age. He abided by the commands of a precious few adults, barring his own folks, and cared little for the concept of authority figures, instead, choosing to heed his own gut.

To further illustrate the boy's lack of respect for authority, as well as the aptitude for lying and scheming he had already developed, there is an anecdote about Ludwig and 12-year-old Lustig. According to the story, the patriarchal Lustig, like many other fathers, had big dreams for his sons – particularly his eldest – and attempted to live vicariously through them. Victor, he hoped, would one day shoot to stardom as a celebrated violinist. Victor's younger brother, Emil, who showed more subtle, but equal promise, would follow in Ludwig's footsteps and become a reputable and successful merchant, and perhaps, one day, *burgomaster,* too.

Not long after Lustig's 12th birthday, Ludwig gifted him a gorgeous violin. The boy clearly possessed a stellar ear for music even as a toddler, instinctively bobbing his head along to any melody with perfect rhythm, and he was not to squander his talents. But much to Ludwig's dismay, his eldest exhibited zero interest in the bowed instrument. Even so, Ludwig guilt-tripped his son into submission and eventually sent him to the home of a relative in Vienna, where he was to take daily two-hour lessons from the most prestigious violinists in all of Austria.

The boy had other plans. Instead of hopping on a train to Vienna as instructed, Lustig journeyed 723 miles west, crossing the borders of Germany and France, and alighting in Paris, where he remained on the loose for two months. The resourceful prepubescent bounced around from one temporary accommodation to another, relying on the hospitality of kindhearted strangers – no doubt armed with a sympathy-inducing story – for food and shelter. His independence only heightened during this trip, as did his people skills, given the colorful cast of characters he encountered along the way, among which was a benevolent brothel Madam who extended to him both free lodging and protection from seedy adults for some time.

His adventure concluded when he got himself pinched by a roaming police patrol, who then escorted him back home. It's easy to imagine the fit his furious father threw when the sheepish Lustig appeared on the front step with his violin, still in its sealed package, tucked under his arm. Ludwig, who was just short of foaming at the mouth, ripped the package apart and bashed him alongside the head with the untouched violin, apparently with such force that it shattered upon impact. The young Lustig eventually complied with his father's wishes and attended violin lessons for a while. When he failed to conjure up even a scintilla of passion for the instrument, Ludwig finally allowed him to discontinue his lessons.

Due to his detachment from the violin, Lustig claimed, his lessons circumvented his otherwise extraordinary powers of retention. This isn't to say that the boy was categorically apathetic towards acquiring knowledge of any sort. Quite the contrary, he showed enthusiasm and excelled in several subjects throughout his school years. Lustig was enrolled in a boarding school in Dresden during the median years of his formal education, which his father – who had by then abandoned his dreams on transforming his eldest into a world-renowned musician – hoped would equip him with the business savvy needed to take over his ventures in the future. Not all hope was lost; if Victor would just buckle down and apply himself wholeheartedly to his studies, Ludwig told him, he could establish himself as an honorable, contributing member of society, which often came hand-in-hand with a windfall of wealth. Victor, it appeared, was only concerned about achieving the latter.

In Dresden, Lustig outshined the rest of his classmates in almost all subjects, but he was especially partial to foreign languages, psychology, and sociology, all of which obviously helped successful con men. Foreign languages were his clear forte, and he went on to learn and master Czech, German, English, French, and Italian by the time of his death. Above all, Lustig was most fluent in German and French.

At the age of 19, Lustig began his short-lived college career at the University of Paris, though what he selected as his major is unclear. Like any other university student, Lustig took the time to explore and foster his hobbies and interests. The violin, for starters, may not have appealed to him, but he was a music lover in general, so he frequented concerts and operas with his friends. He even amassed a private collection of music boxes alongside an assortment of clocks and watches. He never recovered from the travel bug that had bitten him as a young lad, so he continued to travel to different cities, where he enjoyed the sights, attended local events and shindigs, soaked up different cultures, and further refined his social graces by rubbing elbows with people from varying backgrounds. In his spare time, Lustig indulged himself in various recreational activities, such as sailing, hiking, preserving butterflies, and enjoying the company of birds and other small animals at the park.

Above all else, Lustig loved to bury his nose in books, poring over history texts, philosophy and psychology pamphlets, oratory and debate manuals, and any other literature he could get his hands on. Blessed with the gift of gab, the young man regularly engaged in deep, meaningful discourse on a miscellany of topics with peers and professors alike, and when his competitive spirit was invoked, he challenged them to friendly, yet animated debates. He was one of those who seemed to know a little about everything, a skill he practiced with great finesse, and one that would serve him well in his future endeavors.

At the same time, the 19-year-old adopted far less healthy habits and hobbies, spending many an evening in billiard halls, poker joints, blackjack tables, horse and dog tracks, and other sleazy establishments. He threw himself into the world of gambling, and in due time he carved out a reputation as an unflinching, yet astute better. Soon, he began to skip his classes, preferring to consort with his gambling buddies instead.

Lustig occasionally pilfered sweets and other insignificant items like many other mischievous children, but by the second decade of the 20th century, he had officially hoisted himself onto the first rung of the ladder of unambiguous criminality. He started out, similar to many others in his dubious field, as a panhandler, but he was eventually put off by the ignominy and the scant returns. In time, he graduated to pickpocketing, burglary, and street hustling. The young Lustig discovered that he had a flair for card tricks and sleight-of-hand illusions. His profits, in turn, helped feed his growing gambling habit.

Perhaps it was Lustig's tendency for recklessness as a young man and the lessons in humility that often ensued that shaped his capacity for foresight, as well as his skills of evasion. One summer evening, a young Lustig – presumably having imbibed one too many pitchers of beer – approached an attractive woman at the bar of his local pub and began to flirt with her. Whether he was aware of her relationship status is uncertain, but either way, the woman's boyfriend, who soon returned from the toilet, was livid, so much so that he deprived Lustig of a chance for an explanation. The upset lover drew his dagger and pounced on Lustig from behind. The scrappy Lustig stood his ground but was ultimately overpowered by the much burlier gentleman. He walked away from that exchange with a permanent scar on his face, the gash stretching from his left temple to his earlobe, to go along with his bruised ego. Policemen and other authorities who later crossed paths with Lustig frequently referred to him as "the Scarred."

While Lustig would have consistently placed high in all his classes had he truly committed himself to his studies, the formality and tedious predictability of university life in general failed to satisfy his insatiable hunger for adventure and great riches. As a result, Lustig abandoned his formal studies after no more than two semesters and ventured out into the "real world," opting instead to enroll himself in the school of life. "I have never ceased going to school," Lustig later clarified in a letter he penned in prison. "I have a consuming thirst for knowledge and have always been able to find it, one way or another."

Lustig's departure from the University of Paris coincided with the unfolding of the Belle Epoque, the pre-World War I gilded age that swept across Europe and the United States. The "Beautiful Age" in France began shortly after the conclusion of the Franco-Prussian War in 1871, and it lasted until the assassination of Archduke Franz Ferdinand of Austria in 1914, which served as the catalyst to the first global war. It was during this golden era, which brought about the vitalization of iron, chemical, and electricity sectors, paired with the introduction of car and aviation industries, the expansion of railways, and the rise of consumer culture, that the upper and middle echelons of society thrived. The standards of living, as well as profits, and in turn, material wealth, vastly improved among the privileged classes, but naturally, the poor were left behind.

The Belle Epoque bore different names in neighboring countries. In the United States, the Belle Epoque was simply called the "Gilded Age," and in Mexico, it was referred to as "El Siglo de Oro," or "Golden Century," an unlikely period of prosperity that arose during the three-decade dictatorship of President Porfirio Diaz. In Britain, the Belle Epoque encompassed the golden reigns of Queen Victoria and King Edward VII. The rise of the rich, coupled with the progressively conspicuous divide between the privileged and the poor, was a pattern that emerged in all these locations. At the zenith of the American Gilded Age, for instance, the richest two-percent of citizens owned over a third of the entire country's wealth.

Lustig was resolved to keep up with the elite at any cost, and it became something of an obsession that consumed him for the rest of his life. The growingly glamorous lifestyles of the rich and powerful, colored by sprawling, magnificent estates, luxurious suits fit for a prince, opulent banquets, and endless cruises and fancy vacations, served as a wake-up call. If he wanted a slice of that sumptuous pie, he would have to retire his deleterious gambling habit and frivolous street hustles and transition to far grander and more systematic schemes.

The key to Lustig's future riches, he believed, was cupped in the bejeweled hands of the wealthy, most notably the *nouveau riche*.

Cruises, Capone, and the Ten Commandments

"My work is not illegal. I simply find people who are doing illegal things already. I merely assist them to further their illegal acts." – attributed to Victor Lustig

Lustig's first official venture into con artistry took place aboard a number of transatlantic ocean liners. Luxury cruises, otherwise known as "pleasure cruises," were some of the most symbolic hallmarks of the Belle Epoque, a trend that was only further popularized by the unveiling of the White Star Line's spectacular and famously "unsinkable" mega-vessel, the RMS *Titanic*. The British-owned White Star Line was only one of the numerous shipping firms constructing these state-of-the-art floating palaces; other contenders included the Cunard Line, the Hamburg-America Line, and the French Line, all of which competed to outdo their rivals in terms of size, speed, efficiency, and grandeur.

The outstandingly lavish interiors of these massive ships, conceived and engineered by the world's most illustrious architects, were designed to transport passengers to a new, yet familiar, self-contained world, essentially redefining the once uninspiring and plodding voyages of transatlantic travel. The décors of these vessels, as dictated by market research, were reminiscent of the castles and mansions of European royals and aristocrats. Each and every room – barring the quarters of third-class passengers – dripped with opulence and sophistication. First-class common rooms, furnished with plush, richly-patterned carpets and dazzling chandeliers, were equipped with spacious parlors, smoking lounges, writing rooms, veranda cafes, and exquisitely carved grand staircases as centerpieces. Along with bewitching bedroom cabins, which featured splendid canopy beds and antique vanities stocked with expensive perfumes and other toiletries, privileged passengers reveled in the luxury of private bathrooms, swimming pools, and Turkish baths. To top it all off, passengers enjoyed five-star gourmet meals prepared by international chefs, live mood music, dance parties, and gambling sprees, among other round-the-clock entertainment.

This was certainly a world that the bourgeois Lustig could get used to, but even more importantly, these luxury liners were the perfect places to fish for prospective marks. Aboard these ships, first class passengers seemed almost eager to rid themselves of their cash, and the multitude of passengers, along with the hundreds or even thousands of crew members, made it easy for such hustlers to fly the coop and stay out of sight if needed. These passengers cut the rug, regaled themselves with scrumptious dishes and booze, and gambled away to their heart's content, utterly oblivious to the shifty characters lurking in their midst.

Once Lustig had selected his target, typically those who flaunted their pearls and gems and were dressed to the nines, he approached them, but did not strike up a conversation with them just yet. Instead, he posted himself up at a table game and drummed up a small spectacle with his card tricks, all the while refraining from crossing into obnoxious showboating territory. Ideally, such a set-up prompted his victims to approach him, as opposed to the other way around, which brought him one significant step closer to acquiring their trust.

When a conversation was initiated, Lustig presented himself as a modest, but highly intelligent and well-mannered individual. He paid close attention to the dialogue exchanged and dished out compliments without appearing too sycophantic. He never foisted his "profession" unto his victims- it was only when they inquired as to what he did for a living that he mentioned he was a famous Broadway producer with a glittering portfolio who, as it so happened, was on the hunt for prospective investors. He always conducted extensive research on his bogus careers beforehand so as to better flesh out his characters. Furthermore, while his productions were non-existent and therefore required a certain amount of name-dropping and the fabrication of fictional profits, he was careful not to oversell his victims, reeling them in with credible-sounding promises and returns. Of course, none of these investors ever received a dime, and by the time they wised up, the Broadway producer would never be seen again. As creative as the ploy was, it was no more than a two-bit stunt when juxtaposed with his future capers.

His refined skills of persuasion, as well as his surprising knowledge about the world of Broadway, can most likely be attributed to his alliance with the disarmingly suave Nicky Arnstein, who was married to Fanny Brice, a Ziegfeld Follies starlet and muse for Barbara

Streisand's *Funny Girl*. It was reportedly Arnstein, a slick, 6'6" professional gambler and career crook, who mentored Lustig and shared with him his hefty bag of tricks before doubling as his first known partner-in-crime. Precisely how involved Brice was in their schemes is unknown.

Arnstein

Brice

Like Lustig, Arnstein, born "Julius Willard," operated under a slew of aliases, ranging from "Jules Arndtsteyn" and "Wallace Ames" to "J. Willard Adair." "Nicky" was a pseudonym he adopted in the 1890s, inspired by the "nickel-plated" bicycle he owned as a child in Berlin. He, too, started out as a small-time grifter, mainly manipulating street card games and horse races before advancing to larger-scale gambling gambits in exclusive European casinos and on luxury liners. He was a protege of the notorious Arnold Rothstein, one of America's most famous mobsters, whom Arnstein hailed as the "king of gamblers." Rothstein, who was very much responsible for the success of organized crime in early 20th century America, moonlighted as a bookie, loan shark, labor racketeer, Wall Street swindler, and a dealer of illicit goods, but his alleged fixing of the 1919 World Series was unquestionably the highlight of his criminal career. It was through Arnstein that Lustig became acquainted with Rothstein, who, by extension, also imparted much wisdom to the swindler-in-training.

Rothstein

Lustig held great admiration for Arnstein, who was no ordinary scam artist. Arnstein never relied on his gun, or any other weapon for that matter, when it came to stealing from his victims. Rather, he utilized his brains and gumption, befriending his victims and gaining their confidence before fleecing them at table games. It was a smooth and clean operation, there were no lives at stake, and since Lustig had little sympathy to spare for the financial losses of his privileged prey, he considered it a win-win situation.

Lustig and Arnstein's partnership lasted for roughly a year or so, during which Lustig mostly watched with silent awe as his associate worked his victims, studiously taking mental notes and later employing Arnstein's tactics in his own schemes. Meanwhile, Arnstein was impressed by Lustig's sponge-like powers of observation, his fearlessness, and how well he took to constructive criticism. It was from Arnstein that Lustig learned how to maneuver his marks into voluntarily relinquishing their cash. He taught Lustig the importance of appealing to his victims, and he delineated the fine line between flattering remarks and syrupy groveling. If overdone, Arnstein warned him, a more perceptive victim could easily smell a rat.

Arnstein demonstrated this maxim in real-time by inviting Lustig to secretly spectate one of his clever machinations. One evening, Arnstein blatantly revealed to a competitive voyager his actual line of work: a professional con man who manipulated card games for profit. The voyager in question, who fancied himself a superlative gambler, was instantly titillated, and for the next few days, he hounded Arnstein for a game, to which the latter continuously refused so as to keep him wanting. Arnstein finally took him up on his offer on the final evening of the voyage and proceeded to take him for a ride that set him back $30,000 before the dupe could demand a rematch.

The razzle-dazzle of the Belle Epoque was snuffed out by the outbreak of the First World War in 1914. The sobering reality of wartime led to the depopularization of luxury cruises, and with that, it put an end to Lustig's "Broadway" career and cruise shenanigans. After parting ways with Arnstein, he flitted between Paris and Germany for some time, and it is believed he fell under the employment of a local gambling syndicate. Lustig's stint as a syndicate thug, however, swiftly expired when the gang discovered that he had been skimming from the syndicate's pot. His disgruntled bosses gave chase, but much to the chagrin of his former colleagues, the resourceful and elusive Lustig managed to dodge their radar. With the help of a few disguises, he slipped onto a ship en route to the United States.

Despite his successful escape, Lustig did not take this close call lightly. Never again would he reduce himself to an employee or a mere pawn for another man's gain, for the risk far outweighed the rewards. From that point forward, he would be the sole driver of his own undertakings, and he would only join forces with confreres if they agreed to the stipulation that they be equal partners.

Lustig arrived in New York sometime in the later part of the decade, around the time the Great War ended, and essentially as America was on the cusp of the Roaring Twenties and the chaotic years of the Prohibition Era. Indeed, he hoped that the land of opportunity would grant him the opportunity to elevate his craft, but he opted to take things slow. After all, one would not jump headfirst into an unfamiliar lagoon without first testing the waters.

His first order of business was to forge solid relationships with influential figures, as having friends in high places would only serve him well. To his new friends, he introduced himself as "Count Victor Lustig," a scion descended from deep-rooted nobility in what was once the Kingdom of Bohemia. His comprehensive command of his motherland's politics, coupled with his debonair appearance and genteel manners, enhanced his authenticity.

Lustig treasured these friendships not only because he craved companionship (the life of a traveling con artist, as one can imagine, was a lonely one), but also because he appreciated the unspoken mutual backscratching these alliances usually entailed. He found one such ally in Colonel Frederick Stuart Greene, who would later be appointed New York's Highway Commissioner, and later still the Commissioner (or Superintendent) of Public Works.

Greene

The pair first became acquainted about a year earlier in Paris, sometime towards the end of the war. Lustig, as the story goes, was looking to unload one of the two French ladies in his company when he chanced upon Greene, who happily accepted the proposal. The devil-may-care evening, sadly, took a sharp turn when the foursome, who were on their way to a local dance club, were waylaid by one of the girls' boyfriends. Understandably upset, the boyfriend sucker-punched him in the gut, and a raging free-for-all ensued. Bystanders hastened off to alert the nearest police patrol. The colonel had no business being in this part of town, which were strictly off-limits to the General John Pershing's American soldiers. Even so, rather than abandon his troubled new mate and retreat into the night, Greene risked his military rank and his near-pristine reputation – not to mention his own neck – and managed to drag him into an dimly lit alley to safety before the police arrived. Lustig would never forget Greene's minor, yet selfless act of kindness.

In the years that followed, the pair harbored a discreet, but profound friendship. Lustig granted Greene several favors and ran suspect errands for him on the low, and in return, Greene allegedly threw the cops off Lustig's scent. Lustig held the value of loyalty in high regard, or so he claimed. It was not just about fulfilling one's obligations as an intimate. It was only sensible to make his constancy and fidelity known, especially considering the countless victims and enemies he would accumulate over the years. Burning what few bridges he had, Lustig knew, could easily spell trouble.

For the most part, Lustig kept a fairly low profile during his first year in the United States, carrying out more "favors" for his associates than masterminding his own schemes. He traveled from city to city, securing friendships with influencers from both high society and the criminal underbellies of these cities, and diligently absorbing the societal protocols and taboos of these outwardly incongruous, yet often intertwined worlds.

Lustig's excursions took him to Kansas City in late autumn of 1919. While there, he charmed and befriended powerful professionals, some of whom invited him to a gala attended by political heavyweights and newspaper honchos. Unbeknownst to the 29-year-old Lustig, he would meet the love of his life at this very gala.

It was, as Lustig himself put it, love at first sight. He locked peepers with a ravishing young woman, clad in a shimmery emerald-green cocktail dress, with flowing, fiery-red locks and twinkling brown eyes. The young playboy refused to pass up the chance to chat up the stunning beauty, and so he proceeded to do just that. Her name, she revealed to him in a soft, sultry voice, was Roberta Noret.

The sparks and natural chemistry between the pair were undeniable. Lustig was smitten with the beautiful, funny, and delightfully candid young woman, and fortunately for Lustig, his feelings were requited. She swooned over his European accent and old-fashioned good looks, admired his easy-going, yet headstrong nature, and was intrigued by the scar on his cheek. Lustig, Noret concluded, was a worldly and cosmopolitan man who lived and breathed adventure, and he also flirted with danger, which made him, at least in her eyes, the whole package. Noret had arrived at the party as another man's date (Lionel Moise, a local news reporter), but she left the gala with her arm snaked around Lustig's.

Noret's strength and occasionally abrasive character, Lustig learned, most likely stemmed from her rough childhood. When her father died shortly after her sixth birthday, she defaulted to the custody of her two maternal half-sisters, who proceeded to pull her out of school and sent her to work at a nearby laundry shop. The nightmare of the malnourished and miserably overworked six-year-old only came to a close when her paternal half-sister came to Kansas and acquired custody of her.

Her savior, a traveling socialite, whisked her off to different cities across the continent, exposing her to an entirely different lifestyle. Over the years, Noret was educated in and practiced high society etiquette, but her insecurity was ultimately a beast she could not tame. Although she had developed a taste for the finer things in life, as did Lustig, who would spend the rest of their marriage struggling to maintain their lifestyle, she felt inhibited by her lack of a proper education. In other words, she suffered from impostor syndrome.

Their whirlwind romance resulted in the couple tying the knot just a few weeks later. The lovebirds eloped to New York, which, in hindsight, seemed uncharacteristic of the usually cautious Lustig, and exchanged their vows on November 3, 1919. The newlyweds then celebrated the beginning of their union with a honeymoon tour across Paris and other European cities, during which Noret met her father-in-law in Zurich for the first time.

Ludwig did not disclose his true profession to his new bride all at once, perhaps fearing an adverse reaction. Instead, he opted to take a more piecemeal approach. He dropped one such hint on the evening before they departed for their honeymoon. The following, as recounted by the couple's only child, Betty Jean, is what Lustig said to Noret: "I want you to know Buckle, that my work is different from any you have known. I'll have to tell you about it each time I take on a new job. So, when we get to Paris, I'll have to be away from you quite a bit because of my work. But you can shop and buy gowns for yourself, for I want my Buckle to look like a queen at all times."

In Noret's opinion, Lustig was a definite keeper. Her love for him ran so deep that she accepted his unorthodox and highly controversial line of work, and she overlooked all the secrecy involved in his profession with almost no hesitation. She was willing to do anything for him, and whenever the situation called for it, she fulfilled her role as supporting actress to her husband's personas to the best of her ability. An extract from Noret's diary reads, "I would never have wanted to change him, just enlighten him enough to protect him."

Noret was taken aback when she learned that the pair would be posing as a count and countess on their honeymoon. Even so, as the couple were still quite literally in their honeymoon phase, with both parties still working overtime to impress the other, she swallowed her complaints and purchased stacks of books pertaining to the art of conversation, table manners and social graces in different social settings, histories and cookbooks for a variety of exotic, mainly European cuisines and wines, and high fashion. The last thing she wanted was to unwittingly do something out of character and spoil the illusion. Most importantly, she did not want to embarrass or disappoint her husband.

The couple made certain to iron out the details of their backstories before their departure. To compensate for her inability to pull off a convincing European accent, they decided that Noret would play the role of an affluent American woman who had met, fell in love with, and married a Bohemian count during one of her many regular trips to Europe. Noret even made sure to do her homework before traveling to Zurich, reading up on the history, culture, local sights, and cuisine of the Swiss city, as she also hoped to make an impression on the older Lustig.

This was the loving, compassionate, and considerate side of Noret, but it did not take long for the fiercely passionate young woman to reveal her other side. She was an intensely jealous and vindictive individual who was prone to violent tantrums. In fact, Lustig was granted a glimpse of all this on the evening before they set sail for their European honeymoon. When she lamented her concerns about being unable to blend in with the other first class passengers, Lustig gently assured her that she would be just fine, and to observe and imitate the "many other fine ladies on the ship" should she find herself stumped. The mere mention of other women, it seemed, triggered her, for she felt as if she had to compete with actual high-born women for her attractive husband's attention. She fumed, "If that's the way you're thinking – of all the other 'fine ladies' on the ship, then that ends it! I'll throw myself in the ocean and let the fish eat me before I let another woman take you away from me!"

In all fairness, like any other couple, they had their good days. As the old adage goes, distance makes the heart grow fonder, and this proved true for the unconventional couple. Whenever Lustig was out of town, Noret entertained herself with trips to salons, spas, and upscale boutiques, where she treated herself to new dresses and furs, as well as diamond brooches to add to her extensive jewelry collection. With the fat wads of cash Lustig left behind for her, she also purchased plenty of little gifts to surprise her husband with upon his return. Noret appeared to nurse no grievances about the couple's lack of a permanent address, for she enjoyed the swanky hotels and the different luxuries that every new city offered.

Nevertheless, regardless of their obviously strong feelings for one another, the virulence that erupted on their bad days could not be dismissed. Their relationship, overall, was tumultuous and highly toxic, so much so that the pair even called it quits at one point, only to reunite and exchange their vows a second time in August 1925. Nevertheless, their squabbles only worsened, often morphing into full blown, intemperately aggressive altercations.

While the couple had their fair share of problems, to say the least, their relationship hit rock-bottom when Noret, fueled by a blindingly jealous rage, attempted to run Lustig over with their toddler in the backseat. Noret, as she later confessed, had been antagonized by the rumors circulating about her husband, who had reportedly been seen with other women. When the baffled toddler demanded to know why her mother was chasing her father, Noret assured her they were simply playing a game of tag as she revved up the engine.

Predictably, their destructive relationship did not last. The couple finally separated for good when Noret discovered that Lustig had been secretly housing his long-time mistress, a blonde bombshell by the name of Mae "Billie" Scheible, nicknamed the "Queen of the Madames," in the same hotel.

In the meantime, Lustig continued to orchestrate his sordid schemes, which were growing noticeably bolder with each passing year. As a matter of fact, his audacity had evolved to such a point that he attempted to go where no man dared go before him: conning the co-founder and boss of the Chicago Outfit, and a fellow "Scarface." He targeted none other than Al Capone.

Capone

In Lustig's line of work, profits were fickle and highly inconsistent, marked by both avalanches of riches and dismal dry spells. When Lustig was undergoing the latter, he reached out to his old contact, Arnold Rothstein, and requested that Rothstein set up a meeting with Capone. Interestingly enough, one of the greatest ploys of his career was one that he had to implement on the fly, as Capone ended up changing the date of their meeting. The meeting, initially scheduled to take place two weeks after it was set up, was moved up to three days after the arrangement of the meeting.

Capone was justifiably skeptical about the meeting, for he had never heard of the fellow and questioned his intentions (rightfully so), but Lustig was reportedly so charismatic that the jaded mobster lowered his guard in just a matter of minutes. Lustig's urbanity aside, Capone was visibly awestruck by his visitor's walking cane, which, when unscrewed, contained a secret flask filled with fine wine. Capone's lackeys were instructed to inspect all canes for hidden compartments during routine pat-downs from that point onward.

As Capone swirled his walking-cane-wine, he listened intently to Lustig's proposal. Rather than waste his time with disingenuous small talk, said Lustig, he preferred to get down to brass tacks. He presented himself as a seasoned speculator and requested a sizable sum of money – ranging from $40,000 to $50,000, or even $100,000, depending on the source – which he would invest in sure-to-be lucrative ventures. He vowed to double his money in just two weeks (in some sources, two months).

Lustig left Capone's headquarters that afternoon with a briefcase bursting with bills. Instead of investing the money in the non-existent businesses as he had promised, or potentially flushing it away at a local casino, Lustig simply stored the money in a safe in his living room (in some accounts, in the safety deposit box of a local bank, presumably under a false name), and left it untouched. Exactly two weeks (or two months) later, he returned to Capone's office with the money in full and claimed that the ventures had fallen through. Capone was stunned by Lustig's seeming sincerity and professionalism, which was quite a rarity in his line of work. The mobster commended the con man for his "honesty" and generously handed him $5,000 for his "trouble."

Unlike that operation, the majority of Lustig's schemes entailed much more forethought and several days or weeks of planning. In 1922, Lustig, who was in Missouri at the time, paid a visit to the American Savings Bank and expressed his ardent interest in a shabby, decrepit farm that the branch had repossessed. In doing so, he assumed his most famous alias, that of Count Victor Lustig, and related a sorry tale about how his life had crumbled. According to the con artist, he hailed from Austria (as opposed to Bohemia), and his homeland was laid to waste in the Great War. In other accounts, Lustig used the pseudonym "Robert Duval" and told a similar tale of woe. Following the unraveling of his aristocratic lifestyle, the count gathered his family and what was left of his possessions and relocated to the United States, where he hoped to start fresh as a humble farmer.

The farm was, to the bank, dead weight that they were keen to shed. As such, when Lustig proposed $22,000 in liberty bonds in return for the forsaken farm, the bankers eagerly obliged. The cunning con also managed to swap out an additional $10,000 worth of liberty bonds for cash, citing his need for venture capital to sustain the farm until it became solvent. In hindsight, the validity of the bonds indisputably enhanced the legitimacy of Lustig's story, but how exactly he procured these authentic bonds is uncertain. In any case, the bankers were so thrilled to wash their hands of the unwanted property that they neglected to notice the sleight-of-hand chicanery unfolding before their very eyes. It took several hours for the bankers to realize that Lustig had switched the envelopes and slipped away with all the liberty bonds, plus the $10,000 cash, leaving the bank without a single cent.

One would expect the con to hightail it out of town and take cover in the shadows after carrying out such a daring racket, but Count Lustig did nothing to conceal his tracks. A team of private investigators employed by the bank cornered and apprehended him in his hotel room in

New York City (in some accounts, Kansas) shortly thereafter. The practiced table-turner, however, managed to coax the investigators into releasing him. If the bank were to press charges, he reasoned, word would spread like wildfire, resulting in a bank run. In essence, holding him responsible would mean the bank would have to confront the risk of their clients withdrawing their money in droves under the fear of what they believed to be the bank's inevitable and impending shutdown. Moreover, Lustig succeeded in squeezing out another $1,000 from the investigators, apparently to reimburse him for time lost. In other accounts, Lustig demanded the cash in exchange for his silence. Either way, the investigators complied, and Lustig walked away with not only his freedom, but also a fresh bankroll in his pocket.

A few months later, Lustig traveled to Montreal and targeted yet another banker: a Vermont native named Linus Merton. The day before he approached his mark, Lustig paid a local thug to pinch Merton's wallet. The following day, Lustig personally returned Merton's wallet with all its contents untouched. As one might guess, this helped him acquire the trust of the unsuspecting banker.

Lustig, assuming his count alter ego, confided in Merton about the loss of his family fortune during the war before spelling out the details of a foolproof scheme he had concocted. His cousin Emil, Lustig explained, was an employee at a nearby bookmaking establishment and had installed a tap on the telegraph wire used to reveal the outcomes of horse races. Plainly put, Emil could discover the winners of every race before the betting windows were officially closed.

In a bid to get in Merton's good graces, Lustig and his partner placed a few small bets for Merton and made good on their promises. Once their mark had become fully content with their arrangement, Lustig alerted Merton to the sudden and "unexpected" change of plans. Emil's wife, he informed Merton, had fallen gravely ill, and that it was his wife's wish to move back to her hometown to say her final goodbyes to her loved ones. That being said, Lustig and Emil were prepared to place one final bet for Merton, to the tune of $30,000. Needless to say, after handing over that money, Merton never heard from Count Lustig or Emil ever again.

Lustig's wildly successful streak of deception, as well as his uncanny ability to juggle not only his various ploys, but also his wife and mistresses, can be attributed to the rules he gradually composed over the years. The guidelines he set for himself and employed in all his schemes – now referred to as "Victor Lustig's Ten Commandments," were allegedly documented shortly before his death. They are as follows:

1.   Be a patient listener (it is this, not fast talking, that gets a con man his coups).

2.   Never look bored.

3.   Wait for the other person to reveal any political opinions, then agree with them.

4.   Let the other person reveal religious views, then have the same ones.

5.   Hint at sex talk, but do not follow it up unless the other fellow shows a strong interest.

6.   Never discuss illness, unless some special concern is shown.

7.   Never pry into a person's personal circumstances (they will tell you all eventually).

8.   Never boast. Just let your importance be quietly obvious.

9.   Never be untidy.

10.   Never get drunk.

The Salesman

"All men are frauds. The only difference between them is that some admit it. I myself deny it."
– H. L. Mencken

In May 1925, Lustig sailed to Paris once again, this time accompanied by a French-American man named Robert Arthur Tourbillon, otherwise known on the streets as veteran con man "Dapper Dan Collins." This trip had come about as a result of Lustig's most famous con of all.

The idea behind the mother of all ruses came to the enterprising Lustig on one of his slow days. While sipping his coffee and flipping through a copy of the day's newspaper one afternoon, the eagle-eyed swindler happened upon an article pertaining to the Eiffel Tower and the exorbitant maintenance costs required for the structure's upkeep.

The Eiffel Tower, christened after engineer Gustave Eiffel, was originally constructed in 1887 to serve as an entrance arch for the 1889 Paris World's Fair, but the government had no intentions of keeping the structure, which was set to be demolished in 1909. Although the tower is now regarded as one of the city's most prized monuments, the structure was tremendously unpopular in its early years, as the public deemed it a hideous and pointless eyesore. An extract from a local newspaper, *Le Temps,* dated February 14, 1887, complained, "We writers, painters, sculptors, architects, and passionate devotees of the...untouched beauty of Paris, protest with all our strength, with all our indignation in the name of slighted French taste, against the erection...of this useless and monstrous Eiffel Tower...a giddy, ridiculous tower dominating Paris like a gigantic black smokestack, crushing under its barbaric bulk Notre Dame...the Louvre...[and] the Arc de Triomphe..."

The Eiffel Tower

Eiffel

Despite the public's noticeable discontent, the French government chose to keep the tower intact, as the lofty structure proved itself useful in World War I when it doubled as a radio tower that intercepted the messages of enemy German soldiers. By the 1920s, however, the public's fears had been realized, as the neglected structure was rusting and very visibly teetering on its last legs. The author of the newspaper article Lustig spotted explained that officials were struggling to raise funds for the capital required for much-needed renovations, and the article openly wondered why the state had not yet decided to sell the tower.

Lustig straightened up in his chair and waved over his accomplice at once. Together, they hatched a plan.

To start, Lustig rifled through his rolodex and landed upon the contact information of a local counterfeiter known for pricey, but highly realistic documents. He commissioned the counterfeiter to produce for him a fake ID, which granted him the title of "Deputy Director General of the Ministere de Postes et Telegraphes" (the "Ministry of Postal Services and Telecommunications"), the department in charge of public buildings, as well as a stack of "government-issued" stationery. He then authored a series of ambiguously worded, yet credible sounding letters addressed to the top five (in some accounts, six) metal salvaging companies in the city. He invited these firms to his hotel, where they would take part in the bidding of a remunerative, top-secret government contract.

Lustig went above and beyond to solidify the pretenses. He arranged for all the meetings to be held in Hotel de Crillon, a chic and long-standing establishment reputed for its exclusive clientele, especially diplomats and powerful politicians. He invested in a rented limousine, which he used to chauffeur the firm's representatives around Paris, and he plied them with a resplendent spread of food and alcohol. After lunch, he escorted the prospective buyers to the Eiffel Tower itself. Much to his delight, the party incidentally came across a construction crew that had been tasked with surveying the tower, right as they were recording measurements and estimates for fresh coats of paint, among the costs of other repairs. Ever the smooth operator, Lustig explained to the potential investors that the crew had been dispatched to the scene to gauge what was needed for the dismantling of the eyesore, which consisted of roughly 7,000 tons of iron. Without missing a beat, he sauntered up to the crew, flashed his fake ID, and ushered the party into the tower for a private tour.

The Hotel de Crillon

His faithful adherence to Commandment #9 (never be untidy) played a vital role in all of his schemes, but it was especially essential in this particular operation. Lustig's regal fashion sense, along with his well-manicured nails, immaculately styled hair, and perfectly trimmed mustache, only rounded out his credibility. Not even the authorities could deny the effortless class that the con man exuded. "He was not the hand-kissing type of bogus Count," reads an excerpt from a *New York Times* article. "[He was] too keen for that. Instead of theatrical, he was always the reserved, dignified noble man." An unnamed Secret Service agent later described him as a despicable, but inexplicably seductive individual, one who was "as elusive as a puff of cigarette smoke and as charming as a young girl's dream."

Following the private tour, the investors were shepherded back to Lustig's executive suite at the Hotel de Crillon, and it was then that Lustig disclosed to his audience, whose spirits had been thoroughly uplifted by the VIP treatment, that the government was in the process of disassembling the structure. The sly salesman repeated the widely reported negative publicity surrounding the fast-deteriorating financial sinkhole that was the Eiffel Tower, and in his impassioned speech, he quoted celebrated French authors. He cited Guy de Maupassant, who chastised the state for its refusal to "smash [the] lanky pyramid," and Alexandre Dumas, who branded the monument as a "loathsome construction." After much deliberation and number-crunching, Lustig continued, officials had finally decided to take heed of the public's protests, but it was their wish to keep the potential sale of the tower under wraps to avoid any backlash from the public until they had worked out all the kinks and details.

Lustig patiently collected bids from all of the investors, who were anxious to score a veritable mountain of scrap metal for a sweet deal, in the four days that followed. Be that as it may, the con man was more interested in the dispositions of his potential victims, rather than the size of the bids they tendered. Lustig ultimately settled upon Andre Poisson, a bright-eyed and bushy-tailed, but diffident newcomer in the field who was starving for his big break.

To Lustig's initial disappointment, when Poisson returned to his suite for a follow-up meeting, he hinted at his cold feet. His wife, Poisson admitted, was incredibly suspicious about the whole matter and had been attempting to persuade him into withdrawing his bid. Lustig did not falter. What a shame, Lustig mused, for Poisson had outbid his competitors. Poisson's ears perked. Regrettably, Lustig continued, there was still a minor matter to be dealt with.

Lustig had a confession to make. He was, in actuality, no more than an overburdened and poorly compensated civil servant, tasked with wining, dining, and choreographing extravagant excursions for the state's clients. Poisson nodded knowingly, as it did not take a rocket scientist to decipher what Lustig was truly insinuating: he was looking to secure a "commission." Ironically, it was the salesman's pursuit for a bribe that dispelled Poisson's doubts, as it was his belief that all bureaucrats were corrupt, double-dealing snakes. After all, that had always been the way the cookie crumbled. Thus, Poisson agreed to hand over a bonus sum of 50,000 francs, on top of the buyer's original offer of $20,000 francs. All in all, Poisson paid what he believed to be an equitable 70,000 francs, roughly $1 million USD today, for the "deed" to the Eiffel Tower. In other accounts, Poisson coughed up 250,000 francs for the rights to the tower, in addition to 70,000 francs for the commission.

Upon receiving the money, Lustig and his partner, Collins, immediately leapt aboard a passenger ship destined for Vienna. They splurged their ill-gotten gains on glitzy hotel suites, tinseled gastronomic adventures, and enjoyed high-priced ensembles, among other luxuries. In the meantime, they kept an eye out for news reports regarding the brazen scheme, which would most certainly have made headlines, but could find no such article. Poor Poisson, Lustig theorized, was either in denial about failing to do his research and having fallen for what was, in retrospect, an obvious scam, or he was too mortified to go to the press, as the publicity would have undoubtedly inflicted some serious damage on his firm's reputation and stock value. In any event, Lustig was confident that Poisson had chosen to cut his losses and would take the secret to his grave.

Instead of chalking it up to a bizarre stroke of luck and advancing to other ventures, Lustig's arrogance, which had been steadily swelling over the years, led him to return to Paris just six months later. He reached out to a different set of scrap metal dealers and repeated the process, including his speeches, and once again, Lustig succeeded in auctioning off the rights to the Eiffel Tower with the state none the wiser, or so he thought.

Lustig's first sale, as it turns out, had indeed been a fluke. He had misjudged his second mark, who was far more assertive and self-assured. As soon as the mark untangled the hoax, he made his way to the local police department and filed a report, and the sensational news of the phenomenal con, which featured the name and description of the perpetrator, made the front page of all the national newspapers. Lustig, naturally, had anticipated such an event, which was far from his first rodeo. Parisian authorities unleashed squads of police officers across the country in an effort to track down the mountebank, but by then, the slippery salesman had already disappeared into the bustling, faceless crowds of New York City, over 3,500 miles away. The mark could only take comfort in the fact that there would be no third sale of Eiffel Tower, and now that Lustig was a wanted man in Europe, he would not be making his return any time soon, if ever.

Again, Lustig's close call did nothing at all to deter him from carrying on with his perilous and exceedingly precarious vocation. In New York, Lustig commissioned a crooked cabinet carpenter to whittle for him a special box carved out of glossy mahogany, and he placed him on retainer. These mahogany cubes, otherwise known as "Rumanian Boxes," measured roughly 12 inches square apiece and had thin slits carefully incised onto both ends, as well as an array of sleek, high-quality brass dials and cranks. Lustig later bragged, "The box literally paid for itself...and then some."

Lustig, presumably by his lonesome, climbed aboard a train bound for Palm Beach, Florida in 1926, though some say it was as early as December 1925. Not long after his arrival, the swindler came upon a self-made entrepreneur, a fellow hotel guest named Henry Loller, whose once moderately successful business had recently taken a dive. Like the other guests, Loller had been quietly observing the poised mustached man from afar, rumored to be an obscenely wealthy European count often seen gliding in and out of the hotel with great haste – doubtlessly to attend to some important business – and zipping around all over town in his brand-new Rolls Royce, driven by his personal Japanese chauffeur.

Loller could not imagine why such a sophisticated man such as Lustig would take an interest in him, but he readily sprang on the opportunity to converse with royalty. The pair swapped stories. Loller, as he explained, was the founder of a firm that specialized in the production of transmission flywheels. Sadly, large corporations were undercutting him in every which way, and he feared that he would not be able to keep his firm afloat much longer. Much to Loller's astonishment, Count Lustig not only empathized with him, but claimed he could relate. According to Lustig, the contemptible Communists had confiscated his family fortune during the Great War, and since he was too old of a dog to be learning new tricks, he had no choice but to start from scratch. But luckily for him, Lustig added wryly, he had found himself a secret weapon. Loller was hooked, and he pressed Lustig for more information until he "wore him down." It was only then that Lustig invited him to his suite and revealed his mahogany box, which he presented as a "money-duplicating" device.

The wide-eyed Loller watched as Lustig demonstrated the device. The count loaded a single $100 bill into one of the slits, along with a plain sheet of high-rag cotton paper into the other. What Loller failed to notice was a second $100 bill, its serial number doctored to match the original bill, that Lustig had previously inserted into the machine. Lustig then fiddled with the knobs and dials, and the device consumed both the bill and the cotton paper on both sides. Now, all there was left to do was wait, said Lustig, as it took approximately six hours for the cotton paper to soak in the mysterious chemical solution. He warned Loller against opening the lid prematurely, for doing so would impede the transferring of the images.

Lustig and Loller returned to the former's suite precisely six hours later. Once again, Lustig cranked the dials, and lo and behold, two identical bills emerged from either side of the device. To further illustrate the efficacy of his nifty contraption, Lustig brought Loller to a nearby bank and presented the bills to a teller, who deemed the bills legitimate.

Loller was floored. Believing that he had ensnared himself a golden goose of the rarest kind, he begged Lustig to sell him the mahogany device for $25,000 (approximately $400,000 USD today), which Lustig obliged. Loller, under the impression that the machine was the only one of its kind in existence, forked over the cash with great pleasure, since it was seemingly a small price to pay for a lifetime of unlimited riches. Lustig lined his suitcases with Loller's money, checked out of his suite, and left town that same evening. The con artist had expected his mark to figure out the ruse after the six-hour "waiting period," but poor Loller assumed that he had bungled the process and proceeded to flog the dead horse for weeks, allowing Count Lustig to make a clean escape.

Lustig continued his Rumanian Box routine across the country, defrauding impressionable civilians in Indiana, Texas, Chicago, and Nebraska, including a county tax collector who was swindled out of $123,000 in tax receipts. Lustig operated under various aliases, but not all of his marks were quite so naive. A few of them went to the authorities, which landed Lustig in prison at one point. In fact, he shared a cell with a serial bank robber and leader of the Terror Gang named John Dillinger. Still, the hardened confidence artist had no intentions of slowing his roll. When he got out of jail, he headed for Ramsen County, Oklahoma, and zeroed in on one of his most high-risk targets yet.

A few weeks after his arrival, Lustig was thrown behind bars once again, this time for unrelated fraud charges, but instead of accepting his fate, the quick-thinking Lustig paced back and forth in his cell and soon conjured up a plan. Lustig capitalized on his arresting sheriff's surprisingly suggestible nature. That sheriff, S.R. Richards, was dazzled by the arrestee's model manners and clean-cut appearance, as well as his willingness to cooperate upon his arrest. Moreover, he was spellbound by the expert conversationalist's natural magnetism, so much so that he unlatched the lock of the prisoner's cell and poured him a glass of confiscated moonshine, which Lustig, who normally refrained from drinking on the job, presumably sipped politely. After shooting the breeze for some time and chatting about sports, films, and other things, Lustig zeroed in on Richards' Achilles heel: women.

The tipsy sheriff disclosed that he was a frequent patron of the brothels on Bourbon Street in New Orleans and confessed that he was bankrolling the living expenses of a prostitute whom he had taken a shine to. Supporting his inamorata and gratifying her expensive taste, however, had become an unbearable financial burden, and the near-bankrupt sheriff was now $25,000 in debt. Lustig privately rejoiced at this revelation, but he donned his best poker face. He convinced Richards to retrieve the strange mahogany box the sheriff had confiscated during his booking and staged for him a demonstration of the box's magical properties. The sheriff was sold at once, and an agreement was forged. In return for the device, which Richards purchased for $10,000, Lustig would be granted his freedom. It took the sheriff less than 12 hours to realize that he had been duped, but by then, Lustig had already skipped town.

Richards tracked Lustig down in his Chicago hotel room about eight months later. Blinded by fury, the sheriff drew his pistol and shoved the barrel in Lustig's face, but the count had prepared for such a scenario. This was no more than an unfortunate misunderstanding, Lustig coolly explained. Perhaps the box was faulty, or the sheriff had misinterpreted the instructions, but either way, Lustig was prepared to return his $10,000 in full until they worked out the problem.

The count fidgeted with the box for some time, and six hours later, handed the sheriff freshly printed $100 bills. Somewhat incredibly, Richards took him on his word, returned the $10,000, and went on his merry way with the Rumanian Box tucked under his arm. The sheriff was arrested just weeks later in Bourbon Street for attempting to settle his bill with counterfeit bills, and he received a prison sentence, which he later served in a Lewisburg penitentiary. As an agent named Frank Seckler put it, "Victor Lustig was a top man in the modern world of crime. He was the only one I ever heard of who swindled the law."

Catching the Count

"A liar will not be believed, even when he speaks the truth." – Aesop

As it turned out, the end was nigh. Lustig's reliance on his marks' chagrin and their refusal to rat him out in a bid to keep a lid on their own criminality could only take him so far, and his luck was wearing thin. His hijinks had caught the attention of the Secret Service, who were now on the lookout for the two-faced count. A snippet from an article published by the *Chicago Daily Tribune* on February 2, 1933, told readers, "Albany Park police are searching for three men, one a pseudo German chemist, who swindled Frank Wagner...out of $10,000...Wagner met one of the trio, Ray Finalle, last week. Finalle introduced him to the other two, one of them identified as 'Silly Willie,' and the other as Victor Lustig the German Chemist."

In 1930, Lustig partnered with an engraver and pharmacist, William Watts, as well as chemist Tom Shaw, for what would be the last grand scheme of his decades-long career. The trio launched a large-scale counterfeiting operation, utilizing engraving plates, high-rag cotton paper, and special inks that mimicked the minuscule green and red threads in legal tender. The counterfeit cash, which authorities later dubbed "Lustig notes," were flawless to the untrained eye. They were produced en masse, and an alarming $100,000 (roughly $1.4 million USD today) worth of false bills were released each month across various cities, from Chicago to New Orleans, which threatened to compromise the value of the country's currency altogether.

Lustig may have once again escaped had it not been for his wandering eye. Sometime during the winter months of 1933, Lustig's then-girlfriend, Mae "Billie" Scheible, discovered that the two-timer had recently taken Shaw's mistress on a romantic road trip, and to make matters worse, he had used Scheible's Cadillac to carry out his infidelity. As one would expect, the wronged woman blew a gasket and tipped the police off to the location of his headquarters on 74th Street in New York City. The Secret Service assembled an investigative squad and proceeded to tail the count for the next seven months. At this stage, Lustig was no more than a person of interest, because Watts was the man they were truly after. Watts' rap sheet, which included the counterfeiting of whiskey labels and moderate amounts of American currency, rendered him a leading suspect. "Count Victor Lustig" was Watts' only known contact.

The squad, captained by Robert L. Godby, made their move on May 13, 1935, descending upon Lustig in the city's Upper West Side. During his interrogation, the imperturbable con man delivered the name of his partner on a silver platter. Watts was indeed heavily involved with the counterfeiting operation, said Lustig, and while he was aware of the unethical venture, he himself played no role in the scam whatsoever.

The arresting officers, it seemed, were a step away from awarding him the benefit of the doubt until it came time for a routine inspection of the count's belongings. Lustig's suitcase was filled with neatly-folded piles of clothes and a small assortment of toiletries. His wallet, on the other hand, contained a single telltale key, which they later matched to a locker in Time Square's Brooklyn-Manhattan Transit station. Inside the locker were a set of engraving plates cast for $5, $10, $20, and $100 bills, which sat alongside a stack of bills amounting to $52,000.

This time, Lustig had nowhere to run, at least for the time being. Count Lustig was detained and bussed over to the Federal House of Detention, where he would remain until his upcoming hearing. One of the agents on the car ride to the detention center allegedly said, Count, you are the smoothest con man in the world." To this, Lustig disagreed. "I wouldn't say that," Lustig replied in a low voice, void of emotion. "After all, you have conned me."

Those who believed that this was the end of the count's career were sorely mistaken. Rather than wallow in self-pity, Lustig, as restless as he was resourceful, devised an ingenious escape plan. The observant detainee quickly learned that the sloppy attendants were neglecting to keep track of the number of clean linens allotted to each prisoner. As such, in the weeks leading up to his getaway, Lustig collected nine extra sheets and stowed them away inside a slit he had incised in his mattress. Whenever the other prisoners were let out of their cells to stretch their legs, Lustig opted to stay behind, shredding the sheets and weaving together a linen rope.

On September 1, 1935, Lustig claimed that he had fallen ill and requested to sit out the noontime exercises. As soon as the rest of the detainees were escorted to the rooftop, he snuck out of his cell and into the third floor lavatory, where he went to work. He snipped through the wire screening on the windows with a pair of wire cutters he had swiped from one of the guards, and with the makeshift rope tethered to the bar on the window, he slowly lowered himself to the first floor. When he realized that he had an audience – a smattering of pedestrians across the street – he posed as a window washer and pretended to wipe down the windows along the first floor until he slipped out of sight.

Authorities later found the following note scribbled onto a piece of scrap paper on his pillow: "He allowed himself to be led in by a promise; Jean Valjean had his promise. Even to a convict, especially to a convict. It may give the convict confidence and guide him on the right path. Law was not made by God and Man can be wrong." The elusive con had left a quote from Victor Hugo's *Les Miserables*.

Lustig remained on the lam for a total of 27 days. He was eventually recaptured by agents Fred Gruber and G. K. Firestone in Pittsburgh, but not before leading his captors on a wild car chase. Legend has it that when the agents finally caught up to Lustig, who was eventually foiled by a literal dead end, the count nonchalantly exited his vehicle with his hands in the air, making no attempt to resist arrest. With a rueful sight, Lustig said, "Well boys, here I am."

Lustig was branded a high-priority escape risk and placed under extra surveillance. Why the agents failed to do so in the first place is unclear. This was not the first time that the count had broken out from prison - Lustig had sawed off the bars of his cell window in Lake County, Indiana just a few years prior.

Lustig's trial commenced on December 5, 1935. When the prosecutor revealed his former partner, Watts, as their star witness, Lustig must have realized that his fate had been sealed. A recess was called, and shortly thereafter, Lustig went on to plead guilty. Watts was sentenced to 10 or 15 years in prison, while Lustig earned 15 years in Alcatraz. He was given an additional five years for his breakout stunt. By the time of Lustig's conviction, there was an estimated $2.5 million worth of Lustig bills in circulation.

Lustig was also rumored to have been a suspect in several murder cases, such as the shooting death of renowned actor and director William Desmond Taylor, but nothing ever came of these accusations owing to the lack of evidence. Today, the bulk of Lustig's biographers deny his involvement in these murder cases, for such confrontational violence ran counter to his modus operandi.

Lustig's mug shot

A picture of Lustig (right) on the way to Alcatraz

    In the early spring of 1947, a feeble Lustig attempted to request a trip to the prison's clinic. Unfortunately for the serial liar, who had by then filed a staggering 1,192 medical requests, along with 507 prescriptions, his complaints fell on deaf ears. He had become the boy who relentlessly cried wolf, and his once-impenetrable credibility was completely shot. On clinician had written of Lustig that he "is inclined to magnify physical complaints, constantly complaining of...imaginary ills..."

    By the time it dawned on the prison guards that Convict #300 was not faking this time, it was too late. Lustig was transferred to a hospital in Springfield on March 9 of that year, but he would never recover. He contracted pneumonia, as dictated by his death report, brought on by a "hemoplegia probably caused by a left frontal brain abscess," and died on March 11 at the age of 57.

Listed under occupation on his death certificate was "apprentice salesman," a final (and somewhat sardonic) nod to the greatest achievement of his career.

Online Resources

Other 20th century titles by Charles River Editors

Other titles about Lustig on Amazon

Further Reading

Blitz, M. (2015, January 14). THE MAN WHO SOLD THE EIFFEL TOWER. Retrieved March 7, 2020, from http://www.todayifoundout.com/index.php/2015/01/man-sold-eiffel-tower-twice/

Bolt, R. (2014). *The Encyclopaedia of Liars and Deceivers*. Reaktion Books.

Carlson, B. (2020, January 15). What we can learn about modern financial scams from the man who tried to sell the Eiffel Tower—twice. Retrieved March 7, 2020, from https://fortune.com/2020/01/14/financial-scams-lessons-eiffel-tower-sale/

Concliffe, C. (2017, April 11). William Chaloner, Master Counterfeiter. Retrieved March 7, 2020, from https://www.headstuff.org/culture/history/william-chaloner-master-counterfeiter/

Congress, U. S. (1936). *Treasury Department Appropriation Bill for 1937: Hearing Before the Subcommittee of House Committee on Appropriations in Charge of the Treasury Department Appropriation Bill for 1937, Seventy-fourth Congress, Second Session*. U.S. Government Printing Office.

Conliffe, C. (2015, December 14). Victor Lustig, King Of The Con. Retrieved March 7, 2020, from https://www.headstuff.org/culture/history/victor-lustig-king-of-the-con/

Cowles, C. (2019, May 2). How Scammers Trick People Into Thinking They're Wealthy. Retrieved March 7, 2020, from https://www.thecut.com/2019/05/how-scammers-trick-people-into-thinking-theyre-wealthy.html

Dalton, M. (2019, September 17). Smooth Sailing: The Cruise Ship's Evolution From the 1800s to Today. Retrieved March 7, 2020, from https://www.dwell.com/article/evolution-of-modern-cruise-ship-design-5e3aa877

Demain, B. (2012, October 17). Smooth Operator: How Victor Lustig Sold The Eiffel Tower. Retrieved March 7, 2020, from https://www.mentalfloss.com/article/12809/smooth-operator-how-victor-lustig-sold-eiffel-tower

Duval, J. (2018, June 5). The "Rumanian Box" Fraud as Wall Street Metaphor. Retrieved March 7, 2020, from https://blog.bant.am/index.php/2018/06/05/the-rumanian-box-fraud-as-wall-street-metaphor/

Editors, A. I. (2017, November 30). Meet Victor Lustig, The Conman So Smooth He 'Sold' The Eiffel Tower — Twice. Retrieved March 7, 2020, from https://allthatsinteresting.com/victor-lustig

Editors, A. N. (2018). Kings of Counterfeiting. Retrieved March 7, 2020, from http://numismatics.org/kings-of-counterfeiting/

Editors, E. H. (2001, March 12). How do big city shell games and three card monte games work? Retrieved March 7, 2020, from https://entertainment.howstuffworks.com/question590.htm

Editors, F. M. (2013). 10 Fascinating Facts About the Belle Époque. Retrieved March 7, 2020, from https://fiveminutehistory.com/10-fascinating-facts-about-the-belle-epoque/

Editors, F. T. (2015, March 30). How the Eiffel Tower Was Sold. Retrieved March 7, 2020, from https://www.francetoday.com/learn/history/how_the_eiffel_tower_was_sold/

Editors, H. D. (2016, September 14). Victor Lustig: The Man Who Sold the Eiffel Tower... Twice. Retrieved March 7, 2020, from https://historydaily.org/the-story-of-victor-lustig

Editors, H. (2017). History of the town. Retrieved March 7, 2020, from http://hostinne.info/english/ds-1049/

Editors, H. C. (2017). Victor Lustig and Al Capone. Retrieved March 7, 2020, from https://historycollection.co/these-10-historic-con-artists-prove-there-is-a-sucker-born-every-minute/5/

Editors, M. D. (2015). La Belle Époque: The Twilight of the 19th Century. Retrieved March 7, 2020, from https://www.mdc.edu/wolfson/academic/artsletters/art_philosophy/humanities/belleepoque.htm

Editors, O. B. (2018, October 10). The Man Who Sold The Eiffel Tower Twice. Retrieved March 7, 2020, from https://www.offthebeatandtracks.com/the-man-who-sold-the-eiffel-tower-twice/

Editors, P. P. (1951, June 21). The Pittsburgh Press from Pittsburgh, Pennsylvania · Page 19. Retrieved March 7, 2020, from https://www.newspapers.com/image/?clipping_id=37230650&fcfToken=eyJhbGciOiJIUzI1NiIsInR5cCI6IkpXVCJ9.eyJmcmVlLXZpZXctaWQiOjE0Mjk5NzI5MiwiaWF0IjoxNTgzNDg0Mjgy

LCJleHAiOjE1ODM1NzA2ODJ9.VHSlkKA50jX_UbQ5twbUTuhjFcAWE8DKHcULaTCtcW
A

Editors, P. P. (2018). VICTOR LUSTIG. Retrieved March 7, 2020, from https://peoplepill.com/people/victor-lustig/

Editors, S. G. (2015, September 2). Victor Lustig's Ten Commandments for Con Men. Retrieved March 7, 2020, from https://smileandgun.wordpress.com/2015/09/02/464/

Editors, S. H. (2018). Count Lustig – The Greatest Con in the World. Retrieved March 7, 2020, from http://sohpodcast.com/lustig/

Editors, U. I. (2011). For Sale: The Eiffel Tower... Retrieved March 7, 2020, from https://uselessinformation.org/lustig/index.html

Editors, V. (2017, April 24). King of the Con: The Incredible Story of Victor Lustig, the Man Who Sold the Eiffel Tower Twice in the 1920s. Retrieved March 7, 2020, from https://www.vintag.es/2017/04/king-of-con-victor-lustig-man-who-sold.html

Editors, W. (2018, August 28). Drop swindle. Retrieved March 7, 2020, from https://en.wikipedia.org/wiki/Drop_swindle

Editors, W. (2019, April 6). Nicky Arnstein. Retrieved March 7, 2020, from https://en.wikipedia.org/wiki/Nicky_Arnstein

Editors, W. (2020, March 6). Victor Lustig. Retrieved March 7, 2020, from https://en.wikipedia.org/wiki/Victor_Lustig

Emerson, B. (2019, August 28). Atlanta's octogenarian jewel thief, Doris Payne, tells all. Retrieved March 7, 2020, from https://www.ajc.com/entertainment/books--literature/atlanta-octogenarian-jewel-thief-doris-payne-tells-all/Zm0OO1Ys5qld8yXXrl1AvJ/

Emmanual, A. (2016, October 8). Law 12: Use Selective Honesty & Generosity To Disarm Your Victim. Retrieved March 7, 2020, from https://medium.com/@alexanderemmanual/law-12-use-selective-honesty-generosity-to-disarm-your-victim-84763def85ba

Fort, G. (2015, December 14). WHY VICTOR LUSTIG'S CON-ARTIST COMMANDMENTS MATTER. Retrieved March 7, 2020, from https://www.maxim.com/maxim-man/why-victor-lustigs-con-artist-commandments-matter

Greene, R. (2000). *The 48 Laws of Power*. Penguin.

Khederian, R. (2017, June 29). Why Gilded Age ocean liners were so luxurious. Retrieved March 7, 2020, from https://www.curbed.com/2017/6/29/15892518/gilded-age-ocean-liner-history-first-class

King, G. (2012, August 22). The Smoothest Con Man That Ever Lived. Retrieved March 7, 2020, from https://www.smithsonianmag.com/history/the-smoothest-con-man-that-ever-lived-29861908/

Konnikova, M. (2016, April 19). A con artist sold the Eiffel Tower, twice — by listening. Retrieved March 7, 2020, from https://bigthink.com/videos/maria-konnikova-on-the-con-artist-as-listener

Lustig, B. J., & Garrett, N. (2011). *From Paris to Alcatraz: The True, Untold Story of One of the Most Notorious Con-Artists of the Twentieth Century - Count Victor Lustig.* Xlibris Corporation.

Maysh, J. (2016, March 9). The Man Who Sold the Eiffel Tower. Twice. Retrieved March 7, 2020, from https://www.smithsonianmag.com/history/man-who-sold-eiffel-tower-twice-180958370/

Mehrotra, A. (2016, May 5). Here's The Story Of Victor Lustig, The Master Conman Who Sold The Eiffel Tower Twice! Retrieved March 7, 2020, from https://www.scoopwhoop.com/Victor-Lustig-Master-Conman-Who-Sold-The-Eiffel-Tower-Twice/

Origjanska, M. (2017, October 18). Victor Lustig, the smoothest con man in the world, sold the Eiffel Tower–twice. Retrieved March 7, 2020, from https://www.thevintagenews.com/2017/10/18/victor-lustig-the-smoothest-con-man-in-the-world-sold-the-eiffel-tower-twice/

Pietrusza, D. (2011). Arnold Rothstein, Nicky Arnstein, and Fanny Brice. Retrieved March 7, 2020, from http://www.davidpietrusza.com/Rothstein-Arnstein-Brice.html

Prada, L. (2018, January 30). 5 People Who Took Con Artistry To Crazy New Heights. Retrieved March 7, 2020, from https://www.themodernrogue.com/articles/2018/1/29/5-people-who-took-con-artistry-to-crazy-new-heights

Sanabria, S., & Selby, T. (2009). Biography of Victor Lustig. Retrieved March 7, 2020, from http://www.angelfire.com/pro/hoaxes/VictorLustig.htm

Sanabria, S., & Selby, T. (2011). Other Victor Lustig Scams. Retrieved March 7, 2020, from http://www.angelfire.com/pro/hoaxes/OtherVLscams.htm

Scott, C. (2019, September 26). The Art of the Con and Why People Fall for It. Retrieved March 7, 2020, from https://www.psychologytoday.com/us/blog/crime-she-writes/201909/the-art-the-con-and-why-people-fall-it

Shisler, E. (2014, October 10). Victor Lustig ¨ The Count¨. Retrieved March 7, 2020, from https://prezi.com/9aits7uwccsf/victor-lustig-the-count/

Simanaitis , D. (2018, November 15). CONNING CAPONE. Retrieved March 7, 2020, from https://simanaitissays.com/2018/11/15/conning-capone/

Velinger, J. (2003, October 15). VICTOR LUSTIG - THE MAN WHO (COULD HAVE) SOLD THE WORLD. Retrieved March 7, 2020, from https://www.radio.cz/en/section/czechs/victor-lustig-the-man-who-could-have-sold-the-world

Wilde, R. (2019, January 30). Belle Époque or the "Beautiful Age" in France. Retrieved March 7, 2020, from https://www.thoughtco.com/the-belle-epoque-beautiful-age-1221300

Wilson, R. P. (2011). R. Paul Wilson On: The Greatest Con Artist of All Time. Retrieved March 7, 2020, from https://www.casino.org/blog/lustigs-money-machine-scam/

Free Books by Charles River Editors

We have brand new titles available for free most days of the week. To see which of our titles are currently free, click on this link.